A god IN A HUMAN BODY

Tolu' A. Akinyemi

Cover Design: Buzzdesignz

Published by 'The Roaring Lion Newcastle'
ISBN: 978-1-913636-13-5

Email:
tolu@toluakinyemi.com
author@tolutoludo.com

Website:
www.toluakinyemi.com
www.tolutoludo.com

Dedication

To gods who, like me, found refuge in human bodies.

To the most-high GOD.

Table of contents

Acknowledgements

Sincere appreciation to God Almighty – I'm indeed grateful for the wisdom to write my ninth poetry collection and eleventh published work.

A big thank you to my booktiful partner, Olabisi, for always being the first point of call to hear out my poems in their raw state.

To my wonderful children, Isaac and Abigail Akinyemi – I hope someday you grow up to understand your divinity and make your time on this earthly passage worth the while.

Thank you to my wonderful parents, Gabriel and Temidayo Akinyemi – I'm a seed of the divine. Thanking you for the pruning and shaping to the man I am today.

It's an art in itself that a poetry collection would be inspired out of a signing of another poetry collection (*Black Does Not Equal Inferior*) – Adeoluwakishi, a god in a human body. Thanks for inspiring this collection, not by your volition.

To my editors, Adeola Gbalajobi and the Hungry Bookstore – Thank you for being a part of this journey.

To everyone who has supported me on my journey to literary acclaim – your support is greatly appreciated.

POEMS

Dreamland

In dreamland, the demons are breaking sweats,
scampering to safety.
The tear gas of fury stings like a cobra's venom.

They ask, *Who is he?*
Etched on his skin is a two-edged sword,
headstrong with a fiery tongue.

I say, I'm a god in a human body
a broken vessel,
a wandering spirit.

Immerse me in free verses
like flowing rivers.
My tongue levels mountains
then erupts into sparkling joy.

Who dares defy the tempest wind
of a raging god –
a god in a human body?

To dare is to rise

To dare is to rise like snowballs of fire.
O, ye gods, dare and do the unthinkable!

To dare is to rise from the brink
after being dealt life's fatal blow.
O, ye gods, dare and do the unimaginable!

To dare is to rise from the shackles of defeat
to make history.
O, ye gods, dare and do the improbable.

To dare is to rise from every fall
for, you know, rising is a must.
O, ye gods, go and be undefeatable!

My Spirit

My spirit is a lion – indomitable.
My spirit wins battles against all forces at odds with it.

My spirit is on a mission of vengeance,
mouth spitting fire like *Olukoso,*
burning things with strange tongues!

My spirit is a god,
abami eda – strange being.
He wakes every morning, shouting, pacing the room, panting

like a man under a spell.

My spirit is a victor,
winning every battle on his knees!

Olukoso: Yoruba god of thunder and lightning

Marry me

I

Marry me before I say I do to the one
who gnashes her teeth before breakfast.

Marry me before I perish in the ruins of bachelorhood
and my body becomes a wasteland.

II

Marry me before my sad story spreads like wildfire
and my forever happily-ever-after becomes a torrid tale.

Marry me before the clock of my life reaches its menopause
and I become a laughingstock.

Hostage

The bandits have held us hostage with brute force.
Our farms no longer harbour harvested yams.

The bandits have turned our farms
into valleys of corpses.
They say these lands belong to their fathers.

The bandits with no ancestors
have held us to ransom
and our gods are looking on in sheer disbelief.

Rest in Peace

Don't tell me to rest in peace.
My spirit is a bird in flight, restless –
Who sends condolences to the land of the dead?

Don't tell me to rest in pieces.
My spirit needs some peace after the agony on Mother Earth.
Who goes into a needless fight with the dead?

Don't tell me to rest in peace.
My spirit no longer understands the language of mere mortals.
Who will interpret the words of the living to the dead?

Don't tell me to rest in pieces.
My spirit has slept on forever, away from the chaos of the world.
Who dares rustle a spirit at rest?

Curse and Die

They say, curse God and bury yourself alive,
curse and die!
Cry that you erred so you can find peace for your anguished
soul.

Do not curse God in a moment of foolishness,
do not curse your God.

Cry to God,
to cloak you with his garment of mercy
that you may be free from blame,
that he may justify you.

Solemn

I walk in a trance, teary-eyed
My spirit is on a soul-searching mission

My flesh and spirit are in a tussle
The revelations are flooding in
My mind plucks the scattered words like a child
Learning a foreign language
This solemnity is dreamy

Carnage

A writer's den is a carnage,
Taking no prisoners.
Oh, the webs we weave!
The words don't cease.

A writer's heart is a haven.
Invisible darts fly out of control.
Oh, you better believe!
The words rush like waters released.

Mouthpiece

I don't want to be the mouthpiece of an old soldier,
soulless and lifeless.
The god in me has taken prisoners in this raging war.

Breadcrumbs have sunk the brains of men of honour.
They are now without pride –
poverty is a bastard.

I don't want to be the mouthpiece of an old soldier,
clueless and spineless.
The god in me is in a fit of anger at this malady.

Hunger pangs have enslaved the few good ones left;
they have thrown caution to the winds.

I don't want to be the mouthpiece of an old soldier;
bury my conscience with greed,
with a shoulder pad that screams, *Cold Shoulder!*

Mini gods

Three gods are having a nap.
We cried, tried to rustle them from their sleep,
but all we got was silence.
This is the sleep of death.

Three gods are cold, stiff,
buried…
They're on a journey to the land of no return.

To dare is to live

To dare is to hold life by the scruff of the neck
and never settle for good enough.

To dare is to see life from the spectacles of a punter –
victory at the centre.

To dare is to climb the insurmountable mountain and
not capitulate like timid limbs.

O, ye gods,
to dare is to step out of a looming shadow

and live.

Kin and Kindred

Tell my kin and kindred – this body is not my home.
I inhabited it like a treasure, living rent-free,
it never was my own.

Tell my kin and kindred – I was a moving force.
Tell them I was a traveller on the passage of earth,
my spirit wandering like a surfer on sea waves.

Tell my kin and kindred to never settle for less,
for they are from the lineage of warriors.
Tell them that, like me, they are gods
borrowing a human body.

Father of a Queen

My daughter was not born to play second fiddle.
She is a trailblazer charting her own path.

My daughter was not born to be a doormat.
Engrave these words on your patriarchal heart.

My daughter was not born only to be *sucked* in the middle.
She is more than her beyond and behind, more than her curves!

My daughter was not born to scrap her way through life.
I'm the father of a queen, a channel of wealth!

Bloom

Wonder (Wo)man, god
in a human body, bloom
in this raging gloom.

A portrait of a goddess

My imagination runs wild when drawing
a portrait of you, goddess.
You're a deity –
I'm a saint worshipping at your temple.

I'm in awe of a Queen –
calm grace and measured strides.
My imagination runs wild drawing a goddess!

Losing My Mind

I lose my mind, once
in a blue moon. Sparkling
clean like a blank slate.

Abigail

for Abigail, my darling girl

Can I paint you with the precision of Da Vinci,
wash you clean with the morning dew?

You're Gail – hailstorms and thunderstorms –
you're poetry.

Let these words sparkle till you reach your Galilee.
I'm short of metaphors to carve your pristine imagery.

You're the thump of my heart,
you're my spring of joy.

A god in a human body

You're a god in
a human body. Rain fire
like burning coal. Breathe!

Accidental Feminist

I don't need a masterclass in feminism.
My girl-child is the muse
to rain bullets of fury on patriarchal voices.

I don't need a crash course in feminism.
I'm *woke* like a stinging bee on the hunt for honey.

I don't need a tutorial in feminism.
I have birthed a Shero, her own hero.

My girl-child shall cower to no one.

Pray

Erase the shadows
Of yesterday
Deeper than a manhole.

Pray it
Say it
Just one more time.

Wipe out the blemish
Of history
Hanging like dark clouds.

Pray it
Say it
So this won't be a hill to climb.

Expunge the debris
Of the past
That has left the future in peril.

Pray it
Say it
So tomorrow will be fine.

Brown Skin

My brown skin is an
armour. The earth painted me
the colour of grit.

Deranged

Hold the deranged one firmly
before she lets loose more fiery darts

like, *Men are scum*!
Even when they make her *cum*.
Men are crucified till thy kingdom comes.

Hold the deranged ones in their closets
before they are consumed
in the rubble of their misandry.

Hold the deranged one firmly
before they soil you in this muddy fight.

Hold the deranged one firmly
before he lets loose more fiery missiles

like, *Women are inferior!*
Basking in vainglory of faux superiority.
Break these complexes into smithereens,
scatter them to the wind.

Hold the deranged ones in their closets
before they are consumed
in this poisonous misogyny.

Hold the deranged one tightly
before they soil you in these gender wars.

Angry Birds

Seven angry birds on the playground
have bitten more than they can chew. They brought axes
and daggers
to a shouting match,

killed a lion
with claws made of iron.

Seven angry birds on the playground
spit fire and stinging venom. They rain horrors
fresh as morning dew.

In brutal defiance
of the old order, screaming *no more timid silence.*

Spirits

Our spirits have lost focus like a blurry lens.
The drumbeats of war
have left fatal marks on our stainless record.

Spirits are killing spirits.
The open ground is hungry,
swallowing men of steel.

The gods are on the side of the people.
The restless spirits are hunting for blood,
causing damage like a rampaging flood.

Blood-stained streets are haunting shadows.
The spirits have lost their way
in their temporary habitat.

Whore-Ship

The whore-ship is causing commotion in the neighbourhood.
She says, *My body is a map.*
Let them draw, draw on this sinking ship.

Everyone comes and steals more than a few glances.
She says, *My body is a temple.*
Let them in, let them feast with their hungry eyes.

The whore-sheep have lost all sense of virtue.
She says this fight would have no winners.

Run from this *woke* generation before your spirit
becomes a casualty.

Near Death

I missed many arrows of death.
The Englishman says it was a near-death experience.
Driving a speeding car into a brick wall,
emerging like a superhero, unscathed.

That was a cleaner shave than my barber could ever trim.

I dodged many missiles of hate wrapped in fake love.
Father says intuition is a virtue.
My spirit pricks me – that discernment is a gift.

Flood and Fire

The flood that swept the great oak tree was a vicious storm.
Say, *Storm Nancy*.
Why give precious names to these callous winds?

The flood that washed away the fig tree
was a talking drum.
How do we name a barren tree without an axe to grind?

The fires that left California in brazen ruins
were louder than firecrackers.
Why do we hang climate change with a loose tag-hoax?

The fire that turned the Amazon into a dark shadow
was hollow and grave.
How do we open the heavens to scour respite from this
raging heat?

Shade of Love

Our shade of love has changed its colour.
Last night, it was blue and blooming.
Today, it's dark and gloomy.

The red clouds are forebodings of great danger.
Who has the courage to host a foraging parasite?

Our shade of love has lost its enchanting sparkle.
Last night, it was purple and sparkling.
Today, it's pale and frightening.

The dark skies are forebodings of looming danger.
Who will tell these lovesick puppies the end is near?

Toxic

This tune sounds like a strange lullaby.
The ghosts of toxicity are haunting.
This evil wind blowing in the neighbourhood has the scent
of peril.

Tantrums are splitting closed wounds,
stinging fresh scars.
The hail of words is drowning.

In a Human Body

She was a goddess in a human body
In the human body, she was a goddess

She was a spirit in a human body
In the human body, she was a spirit

He was a saint in a human body,
A saint knighted with sainthood

He was a priest in a human body
A priest knighted with priesthood

Searching

I'm on the lookout for a god in a human body – angelic.
My spec is reserved, cool headed
and peaceful, like the ocean asleep.

Sacraments

The sacraments on this altar are not for sale.
Spill the truth like land eroded.

The sacraments on this altar have turned the cattle herds
into the sea of perdition.

Rain woe unto these children of destruction.

The sacraments have been turned into fiery instruments.

My tongue is firing precise shots at targets,
blowing hot air like a fan out of order.

The sacraments on this altar are a sinking hole of darts
and missiles from haunting forces.

Divinity

The macabre dance is a stem of ignorance,
timid souls planting evil seeds.
The whirlwind of sorrow – a tumultuous harvest.

The divine cannot be crushed by
mere mortals.

Evil chants are a sign of grave danger.
The gods are angry.
What gods? What anger?
Who dares wrestle with the divine?

This battle steals peace and causes a ruckus of despair.

Religion

The white man took away our tradition
and left us with his religion.
The seeds they have sown
yielded humongous sorrow.

The black man wears religion like his second skin –
more Christian than the Pope.
Never say *holier than thou.*

The black man's religion is blood thirsty –
holy wars, seventy-two virgins
served as a meal for a gory conquest in a paradise of orgies.

The white man's religion has left us on the precipice,
broken and shattered.

Indomitable Son

for Isaac A, Son of the Lion King

Indomitable son of the roaring lion –
soar, eagle, soar in roaring triumph.
Ascend to the throne of your father's;
atop this hill shall be greater honours.
Climb to the summit and birth a new horizon.

Arise from this looming shadow in defiance,
kingly heir to the great giant,
indomitable son of a great warrior,
nullify the invisible forces of hate forming a barrier.

Yesterday's sour taste is forever buried.
Emerge from the doldrums, merry
majestic robes fit for this vacant throne.
Indomitable son of the great writer, you're not alone.

Shero

for all our Sheroes, we will never forget

Goosebumps of mother's love
send me into the high heavens.
This was more than threadbare.

Paint mother on a canvas – say, *shero*.
This love suffocates more than Cupid's arrows.
I feel the weight sinking into my bone marrow.

Goosebumps of mother's love
drive me into ecstasy.
This sends me into overdrive –
mother's love leaves me in awe – just call her shero.
Her voice echoes,
refreshes my soul like a spring meadow.

Sweet Mother,
Shero,
never forget.

Stories

Beneath her eyes were
tears – rock bottom. Her eyes
tell hidden stories.

How would you draw God's portrait as a poet?

God was a poet who needed no metaphors
or imagery to drive home his point.
Every poet's dream is a lullaby of
words.

God's spoken word – a cheerful delight.
How do you draw a portrait of God
as a poet?

Speak words, create, birth a revival.
Bring to life the dead things.
Bathe in the ocean of words and be still.
These words shape your world.

These creative words are a spring in my
step.
On this spoken-word altar,
God has no rival.

Here's the trivial –
how would you draw a portrait of God
as a poet?

A spoken word artiste –
a verse-spilling page poet or
a creative artiste.

Which of his words would be your favourite
verses?
Would you speak in parables
or tongues of fire?

Tell me,
how would you draw a portrait of God
as a poet?

Choice

for National Poetry Day 2021

Yesterday's choices have grown thorns.
Sinking like a deep gully – the brutal feeling.

Today's choices are deliberate
and delicate –
like fragile china about to break.

Make it cry.
Weep a river of regret
at those fickle choices

that seek to darken
my shining star.

Make it burn,
burn down the tree of indecision
and wrong choices

seeking to consume
my bright future.

Wonder Woman

I'm from the lineage of wonder women.
Women working wonders – Amazons.

I'm from the lineage of wonder-working women –
storytellers!

The hegemony of greatness.
Christie painted stories clouded in mysteries
that left me dreamy,

took me on a sojourn to memory lane.
These days, I chew on those memories in solitude.

Goddess of Love and War

for Olabisi – MJOIV

Our love was smooth as silk –
then it became splintered glass
with visible cracks.

Our love was heavenly –
then the gates of hell brought
a vicious storm.

Our love is standing taller than a twin tower.
What a sweet melody!

Oh, rugged love, firm
against wear and tear
like a durable tyre.

The furnace of love in your veins
runs like a stream,
goddess of love and war.

Let these bodies burn in unrequited love.
Let the flame of love enrapture our soul
so we can birth more poetic days.

Thankful

inspired by Nick Morrison

The world was losing steam like a car engine
overheating on the motorway.
The sound bites from the news were jarring.

Apocalypse came and looked the other way.
We burst into a bubble of sparkling joy.
This revival will have no losers.

We are thankful for the blue skies – still blue.
The sunshine – breaking into a bubble of delight.
The moon rays – our basket of hope.

The evil winds did not break us.
We are the unbroken generation
who survived a raging pandemic.

This nostril blowing light winds
is calming like the sea.

Pause and reflect.
Pause and cry,
cry and pause.

Cry a bucket,
cry tears of joy.
Cuddle your tears.

Hope is here at last.
Hope was never lost.
Can't you see the connecting dots

that kept our lights aflame?
I can see the flame in your eyes,
the sheer joy erupting
like a volcano.

The beam of thanks pouring down
like rain from the heavens.
This poem would wrap itself in gratitude,

breaking forth like spring fountains.
Immerse yourself in gratitude
with a roaring scream of thanks.

A new beginning is here.
New beginnings like no other,
birthing possibilities fresh as the morning dew.

This cup of thanks needs no sweeteners.
These words on the page will resonate
for a lifetime.

How we chose the chorus of gratitude,
rather than sink under the throes of
defeat.

Ocean of Thanks

inspired by ACN Menti – Thankful Fridays

Drown me in the ocean of thanks,
a river overflowing its banks.
Can we just be thankful
for longer days under the sun?

There are days we feel grounded
like a malfunctioning lift,
but this ocean of thanks is ever flowing.

Being among the lucky ones
is sacred protection from God.

Can we just be grateful for health?
The calmness of life,
enough mental strength
to wade through the foraging storms?

On thankful Fridays, dog walking in the park,
we are thankful for the sun rays breaking,
our faces breaking out in bubbles of laughter
as we start a new chapter.

Bio

Tolu' A. Akinyemi (also known as Tolutoludo & Lion of Newcastle) is an award-winning Nigerian author in the genre of poetry, short story, and essays, which include: *Dead Lions Don't Roar* (Poetry, 2017), *Unravel Your Hidden Gems* (Essays, 2018), *Dead Dogs Don't Bark* (Poetry, 2018), *Dead Cats Don't Meow* (Poetry, 2019), *Never Play Games With The Devil* (Poetry, 2019), *Inferno of Silence* (Short Stories, 2020), *A Booktiful Love* (Poetry, 2020), *Black ≠ Inferior* (Poetry, 2021), *Never Marry a Writer* (poetry, 2021), *Everybody Don Kolomental* (Poetry, 2021) and *a god in a human body* (Poetry, 2022).

Tolu' has been endorsed by the Arts Council England as a writer with "exceptional talent". A former headline act at Great Northern Slam, Crossing The Tyne Festival, and Feltonbury Arts and Music Festival, he also inspires large audiences through spoken word performances. He has appeared as a keynote speaker in major forums and events and facilitates creative writing master classes to many audiences.

His poems have appeared in the 57th issue (Volume 15, no 1) of the *Wilderness House Literary Review*, *The Writers Cafe Magazine* Issue 18, GN Books, Lion and Lilac, and elsewhere.

His books are based on a deep reality and often reflect relationships and life and features people he has met in his journey as a writer. His books have inspired many people to improve their performance and/or their circumstances. Tolu' has taken his poetry to the stage, performing his written word at many events. Through his writing and these performances, he supports business leaders, other aspiring authors, and people of all ages interested in reading and writing. Sales of the books have allowed Tolu' to donate to charity, allowing him to make a difference where he feels its important, and to show that he lives by the words he puts to page.

He is a co-founder of Lion and Lilac, a UK-based arts organisation and sits on the board of many organisations.

Tolu' is a financial crime consultant as well as a Certified Anti-Money Laundering Specialist (CAMS) with extensive experience working with leading investment banks and consultancy firms.

He is a trained economist from Ekiti State University, formerly known as University of Ado-Ekiti (UNAD). He sat for his master's degree in Accounting and Financial Management at the University of Hertfordshire, Hatfield, United Kingdom. Tolu' was a student ambassador at the University of Hertfordshire, Hatfield, representing the university in major forums and engaging with young people during various assignments.

Tolu' Akinyemi was born in Ado-Ekiti, Nigeria and lives in the United Kingdom. Tolu' is an ardent supporter of Chelsea Football Club in London.

You can connect with Tolu' on his various social media accounts:

Instagram: @ToluToludo
Facebook: facebook.com/toluaakinyemi
 Twitter: @ToluAkinyemi

Author's Note

Thank you for the time you have taken to read this book. I hope you enjoyed the poems in it.

If you loved the book and have a minute to spare, I would appreciate a short review on the page or site where you bought it. I greatly appreciate your help in promoting my work. Reviews from readers like you make a huge difference in helping new readers choose the book.

Thank you!
Tolu' Akinyemi

Dead Lions Don't Roar

In a society where moral rectitude is increasingly becoming abeyant, Akinyemi's bounden duty is to reawaken it with verses. He, thus, functions as a philosopher-poet, a kind of factotum inculcating wisdom in different facets of life. Dead Lions Don't Roar leads us into the universe of an exact mind rousing the lethargic from indolence or prevarication, bearing in mind that the greatest achievers are those who take the bull by the horn. Taking a step can just be the open sesame to reach the stars. Enough of jeremiad! - **The Sun**

Dead Lions Don't Roar, a collection of poetic wisdom for the discerning, makes an interesting read. A paper pack, the poems are concise, easy to digest, travel friendly and express deep feelings and noble thoughts in beautiful and simple language. **-The Nation**

Akinyemi's verses are concise, straight-edge and explanatory, reminiscent of the kind of poetry often churned out by Mamman J. Vatsa, the late soldier and poet. **–yNaija**

Dead Lion's Don't Roar is a collection of inspiring and motivating modern-day verses. Addressing many issues close to home and also many taboo subjects, the poetry is reflective of today's struggles, and lights the way to a positive future. The uplifting book will appeal to all age groups and anyone going through change, building or enjoying a career, and facing day to day struggles. Many of the short verses will resonate with readers, leaving a sense of peace and wellbeing.

Dead Cats Don't Meow

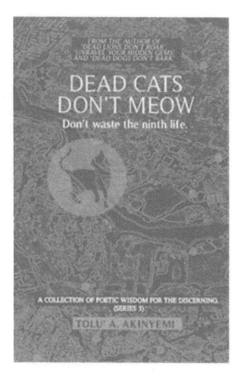

In all, this poetry collection *Dead Cats Don't Meow* generally emphasizes the theme of self-belief and taking action. It reminds me of the saying "if you think you are too little to make an impact, try staying in a room with a mosquito." **- BellaNaija.**

Overall, *Dead Cats Don't Meow* comes across as a collection of thoughtful poetry that inspires, entertains, and educates its reader. It is a great blend of themes spanning across love, inspiration, politics, entrepreneurship, marriage and life, among others. Its simplicity eludes intentionality, and the plays on words show experience.

The collection is suitable for both the literary and non-literary community and is a great work for all manner of readers. I believe, with this one, Akinyemi has achieved his goals of motivation.

- The Nation Newspaper.

Dead Cats Don't Meow urges its readers not to waste their ninth life...the author of the collection of poetic wisdom for the discerning adds his third compendium of poems to the bookshelves alongside *Dead Lions Don't Roar* and *Dead Dogs Don't Bark*. Tolu A. Akinyemi, renowned poet, author and performer, brings to us *Dead Cats Don't Meow*, a metrical masterpiece which invokes love and respect for life with every word. Each poem examines a part of life, a sensation, a reaction, or an emotion. Beautifully written...individually, the verses breathe their own beat, whilst the collection knits together perfectly to present an idyllic collection to attain innate potential. "Don't waste the ninth life! Don't miss the chance to add this rare compendium of poetic wisdom to your bookshelf today!"

Unravel Your Hidden Gems

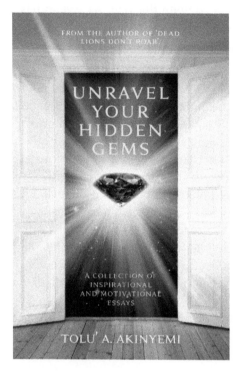

Unravel Your Hidden Gems is like a Solomon talking to us in the 21st century. The book teaches us to value what we have, the pursuit of excellence, and, above all, steps to unravel your hidden gems, drawn from your extraordinary talents, deposited in you right from the first day the placenta was severed from the womb. A book for all seasons, no doubt, especially in Africa where aspirations sometimes do not match inspirations, it is only logical that you add it to your shopping cart. - **Guardian Arts**

Watching others ascend the totem pole of life with relative ease, some come to believe they can't fly. Times without number, they have tried, yet they have found no way to break the ice. Don't despair if you are unsettled by a losing streak.

Tolu Akinyemi, the author of *Unravel Your Hidden Gems,* believes that the hero lies in you. If only you can discover the hidden gems in you, you are on your way to excelling. How, then, do you dig deep into the labyrinth for the gems?

Unravel Your Hidden Gems is a 376-page book by a prolific UK-based Nigerian author. It is a collection of over 360 inspirational and motivational essays from a young man who feels he has a mission to rouse dampened spirits to make the much-needed push in life to regenerate abundantly.

In seven parts, the author makes a diligent search into typical problems encountered by men, capable of weighing them down, and comes up with snippets of wisdom. **- The Sun**

Unravel your Hidden Gems is a collection of inspirational and motivational essays from the heart of the acclaimed author, Tolu' A. Akinyemi. Released hot on the heels of Tolu's first book of poetry, *Dead Lions Don't Roar*, this new book is a study on Life, encouraging people to succeed at what they feel is important to their own happiness. Be it private life, business, religion, career, or relationships, each part of life is discovered. This mind-altering life manual can be read as a whole or visited in snippets for day to day inspiration. Each essay examines and highlights challenges in life and how to succeed in enjoying life with grace. A self-help study on life with a refreshing difference, the book is a totality of life's journey, reminding us we are here on a temporary basis and that it is our duty to not hide in obscurity, but to Unravel Your Hidden Gems before it is too late! Pure Inspiration!

Dead Dogs Don't Bark

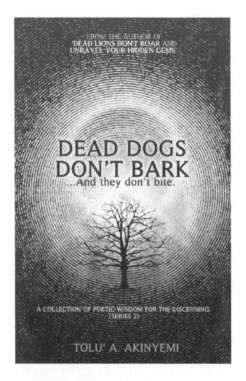

Dead Dogs Don't Bark is as culturally relevant as can be, and this deserves commendation. – **Bellanaija**

In a nutshell, Dead Dogs Don't Bark is enjoyable, it is stimulating. **- Bdaily UK**

The collection takes this reader through an exhilarating journey of wits and pun. The power of words, both grand and subtle, is that it allows the reader to place himself in the scheme and feel the poems on a more visceral level. Creating concrete imageries, the poet says even before it sticks out its tongue and bares its teeth, the first thing that defeats a fainthearted in an unfamiliar threshold is the bark of a dog. It sends cold shivers running down the spine. That very bark, disarming as it is, is the dog's way of calling attention: I am here! - **Guardian Arts**

Dead Dogs Don't Bark is the second poetry collection from the acclaimed author Tolu' A. Akinyemi. With a similar tone and style *to Dead Lions Don't Roar* (Tolu's first poetry collection) this follow-up masterpiece is nothing short of pure motivation. The poems cover a range of topics that many in life are aware of, that the Author himself has experienced and that we all, whatever our age, need support in.

Beautifully written, the poems speak volumes to all age groups as they feature finding your inner talent and celebrating your individuality and distinct voice. The poetry collection has didactic elements for evaporating the effects of peer pressure and criminality amongst many others. Also covering mental health, relationships, career focus, and general life issues, the poetry is bittersweet, amusing, and thought-provoking, in turns.

Never Play Games With The Devil

TOLU' A. AKINYEMI

NEVER PLAY GAMES
WITH *The* DEVIL

Reflective, insightful, and ultimately inspirational, *Never Play Games with the Devil* is a collection best digested slowly and thoughtfully. It's a series of insights and admonitions about life's purposes and coping mechanisms for *"...not crashing under the weight of the world."*
D. Donovan, Senior Reviewer, Midwest Book Review

Readers will find Akinyemi's reflections on significant life issues completely relevant, sharply logical, and deeply felt. -
The Prairies Book Review

Hear the poet as, in a succinct moment of self-adulation, he writes:

"My brain thinks faster than my words can convey.
My mind works magic. Can I live this life forever?"

Divided into three sections, *Never Play Games with the Devil* showcases a poet at the height of his powers, exploring several themes in different voices.

In the first section, the poet is the charismatic preacher encouraging people to Hustle, Find their Feet and Grow. He writes about the lot of Broken Men crashing under the weight of expectations; he talks about boys like Eddie and Edmund, bullied for the shape of their heads. He humorously addresses the consequence of choices in the title poem, 'Never Play Games with the Devil.'

The second section secures him a seat as an activist. We see the poet tackle, in verse, despotic and undemocratic governments, marauding killer herdsmen, and the pastor who lost his voice. The poet mourns the hapless souls in the crossfire between society's rot and the State's insouciance.

The final poems explore the basis of human relationships. The poems here deal with love, commitment, and trust.

Never Play Games with the Devil is a didactic collection of poems on pertinent life issues. These poems draw their appeal from the poet's ability to sustain a figment of thought through the entire span of each poem.

A Booktiful Love

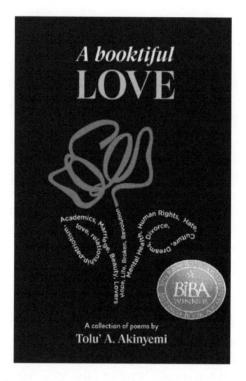

Poet Tolu' A. Akinyemi tackles life with a passionate, analytical, observing eye and creates admonitions which pull at emotional strings in the heart. Poetry readers who choose his free verse collection will find it equally powerful whether it's considering divorce and grief or the love language of 'A Booktiful Love'. **- D. Donovan - Senior Reviewer, Midwest Book Review.**

Readers will find Akinyemi's collection an intriguing approach to exploration of the entirety of human experience in its various forms. This is a superb collection. **- The Prairies Book Review.**

A Booktiful Love is a collection of poems that deal with the entirety of human experience in its various forms. Didactically rich, the poems explore ideas ranging from love, relationships, and patriotism to marriage, morality, and many other concepts pertinent to daily living.

Given its variety of themes, what unifies the poems in this collection is the simplicity and ambiguousness of language which the poet employs. The poems draw their strength from their clarity and meaning.

These are poems with a purpose. Poet Tolu' A. Akinyemi didn't shy away from this fact, as he wrote in the poems "Writers" and "Write for Rights." The poet's philosophy is evident in this collection. To him, a writer is saddled with the responsibility to use his words to teach, preach, and fight for freedom.

He writes:

"Let's change the world, one writer at a time, Write those words till the world gets it right."

Another special attribute to this collection is the poet's experimentation with words. This is clear right from the title. The poet identifies himself as a creator of words. The reader is obliged to travel into the mind of the writer in each poem, to understand how his mind works. As readers approach the end of this collection, they not only become engrossed in its didactic richness, but also will appreciate the uniqueness of the poet's style and the sense of responsibility he carries.

Inferno of Silence

Inferno of Silence is a wide-ranging collection that tackles different themes of love, life, interpersonal relationships, and social and political challenges. It's a hard-hitting, revealing collection that keeps readers engaged and thinking with each short exploration of characters who confront their prejudices, realities, and the winds of change in their lives.

Readers of literary explorations that include African cultural influence and modern-day dilemmas will find this collection engrossing. - **D. Donovan, Senior Reviewer, Midwest Book Review**

Poignant and honest...

Akinyemi's first collection of short stories dazzles with elegant prose, genuine emotions, and Nigerian cultural lore as it plumbs both the socio-cultural issues and the depths of love, loss, grief, and personal trauma. Lovers of literary fiction will be rewarded. - **The Prairies Book Review**

The first collection of short stories by this multitalented author entwines everyday events that are articulated in excellent storytelling.

The title story "Inferno of Silence" portrays men's societal challenges and the unspoken truths and burdens that men bear, while "Black lives Matter" shows the firsthand trauma of a man facing racism as a footballer plying his trade in Europe.

Stories range from "Return Journey" where we encounter a techpreneur/ Poet/Serial Womanizer confronting consequences of his past actions, to "Blinded by Silence," where a couple united by love must face a political upheaval changing their fortune.

These are completed with stories of relationships: "Trouble in Umudike" – about family wealth and marriage; "Everybody don Kolomental" where the main character deals with mental health issues; and "In the Trap of Seers" when one's life is on auto-reverse with the death of her confidante, her mother, as she takes us through her ordeal and journey to redemption. This is a broad and very inclusive collection.

BLACK ≠INFERIOR

Akinyemi employs a steady hand and heart to capturing Black lives in various nuances, from political and social arenas to personal experience: *"Equality is a forgotten child. The blood of the innocents/soil the World. Racial Injustice walks tall,/the graves of our ancestors quake in anguish/at this perpetual ignominy."*

This juxtaposition of the personal and the political makes *Black#Inferior* a particularly important read. It holds a compelling, accessible message to the Black community in the form of hard-hitting poems which offer emotional observations of the modern state of Black minds and societies around the world.

Poetry readers interested in the fusion of literary ability and social inspection will appreciate the hard-hitting blend of both in *Black#Inferior,* which is recommended reading for a wide audience, especially students of Black experience.- *D. Donovan - Senior Reviewer, Midwest Book Review.*

A celebration of black culture and experience and life in general, the collection makes for an electrifying read. - *The Prairies Book Review.*

Black ≠ Inferior is a collection of poems divided into 2 parts. The first part is a collection of thematically linked poems exploring Blackness and the myriads of issues it attracts. The second part oscillates themes— talking about consent, a query of death, a celebration of love among others. In his usual stylistic, this collection deals with weighty matters like race and colourism with simple and clear language.

In Black ≠ Inferior, we see Tolu' Akinyemi reacting in response to the world, to issues that affect Black people. Here, we see a poet shedding off his burdens through his poems; hence, the beauty of this collection is in the issues it attempts to address. In this collection, Tolu' wears a coat of many colours – he is a preacher, a prophet, a doctor and a teacher.

We see Tolu' the preacher in these lines:
'I wish you can rise through the squalor of poverty and voices that watercolour you as under-represented. I wish you can emblaze your name in gold, and swim against every wave of hate.'

This is a collection of poems fit for the present narrative as any (Black) person who reads this collection should beam with confidence at the end. This is what the poet sets out to achieve with his oeuvre.

NEVER MARRY A WRITER

Ultimately, the poet's caution to "Never Marry a Writer" is a deeper disclaimer, a warning that is more a promise. Writers, these poems remind the reader, bear witness. Whether evocative prose or colorful whimsy or the bleakest of forthright documentation, their words attest to the truths they observe. With its wily wordy ways, this collection reminds readers that even those without a literary spouse are nevertheless subject to--and on notice from--those who, like the author, observe and document. --- "The US Review of Books" (RECOMMENDED by the US Review)

"Bold, wry, and lyrical musings." -- *Kirkus Reviews*

OH, THE WEBS WE WEAVE...

For his seventh poetry collection, Tolu' has turned his
attention to that old adage -
no one in a writer's life may have secrets.
A vibrant, human exploration of the way in which words and
deeds connect all of us, and the tiniest movements which
span out across continents.

Tolu' writes powerfully on family, love, loss, and with a
scorching curiosity for the world around us. His readers will
be familiar with his inimitable style, and this latest collection
does not disappoint.

EVERYBODY DON KOLOMENTAL

At its core, the work is simply authentic and resonates both for its content and style. Delivering an almost lyrical sensation with the combination of smaller stanzas, the author's poetry references a multitude of life circumstances, including but not limited to middle school, therapy, and bachelorhood. Filled with poems that unveil a new gem of realization upon each subsequent reading, Akinyemi's poetry is a sure-fire must-read. --- "The US Review of Books" (RECOMMENDED by the US Review)

A poignant collection that captures both the raw sorrows and joys of human existence.... --- "The Prairies Book Review"

Hope is Not Far Away...

Everybody Don Kolomental is a collection of poems that deal with everyday universal struggles.

Tolu' peddles hope to the lost and hopeless and pulls at the emotional strings of the heart in this collection of heartfelt poems. The collection mirrors life through the eyes of a deep-thinker and wordsmith.

Poet Tolu' A. Akinyemi knows the gravity of mental health struggles and uses his words as a soothing balm to heal readers of this collection.

In the poem titled 'Hope is not Far Away', he writes:

"Who will tell Okikiola that hope is not far away?

Its ship docked in the home of Akinyele before his candle was blown out and his flailing dreams were a shipwreck.

Who will tell Okikiola this is not the last straw?

These wind gusts would give way for the calming sea."

Whether you're in need of calm after the storm, therapy, healing, or to view everyday struggles from the lens of a veteran poet, this collection is for you.